The Lost Railways of the Scottish 1

by
Gordon Stansfield

Kelso Station.

Mr & Mrs Dickson of the station house at Shankend.

© Gordon Stansfield, 1999
First published in the United Kingdom, 1999,
by Stenlake Publishing, Ochiltree Sawmill, The Lade,
Ochiltree, Ayrshire, KA18 2NX
Telephone / Fax: 01290 423114

ISBN 1 84033 084 8

PICTURE ACKNOWLEDGEMENTS

The publishers wish to thank the following for supplying the photographs
in this book: Hugh Brodie for pages 5, 7, 17, 20, 26, 30, 31, 37 and 47; W.A.C.
Smith for pages 4, 12–14, 38 and the back cover; and Neville Stead for pages
1, 3, 8, 11, 16 (photograph by P.B. Booth), 18, 22, 24, 25, 29, 32 (photograph by
G.M. Staddon), 33, 34, 35 (photograph by P.B. Booth), 36 (photograph by
P.B. Booth), 42, 43 and 48 (photograph by P.B. Booth).

INTRODUCTION

The Border counties of Roxburgh, Selkirk, Peebles and Berwick are steeped in railway history. The North British Railway Company reached Berwick-upon-Tweed from Edinburgh in June 1846 and throughout the years it was this company that developed the railway in the Tweed towns. Without it towns such as Hawick and Galashiels would not have developed as quickly as they did. Local prosperity was increased and new markets for local products such as those from the woollen mills were opened up far and wide.

As well as local freight, passenger traffic was also an important source of revenue to the North British. The main route through the Borders was the Waverley line which linked Edinburgh with Carlisle. This route opened in 1862 and provided services to and from England until its closure, including through services between Edinburgh and London via Hawick. South of Hawick the Waverley route traversed bleak countryside which was sparsely populated. The most remote station on the line was Riccarton Junction which, as its name implies, was the junction for a cross country line to Hexham and Newcastle. A true railway village, the only access was by rail and there was even a branch of the Co-op on the station platform.

Border crossings into England by rail were at Kershope Foot on the Waverley line, Carham on the line from St Boswells to Tweedmouth, Deadwater on the line from Riccarton Junction to Hexham and at Lamberton on the east coast main line between Dunbar and Berwick, the latter being the only one still in use today.

By the latter part of the nineteenth century most border towns had a rail service. There were branch lines to Eyemouth, Jedburgh, and Selkirk as well as routes serving Galashiels, Peebles, Melrose, Kelso, Lauder, Duns and Berwick. The last rail route to open was the branch to Lauder and ironically this was one of the first to close.

By the 1940s, passenger levels had dropped considerably and the writing was on the wall for the Border lines. The Peeblesshire branch to Dolphinton lost its passenger service in 1933 but it was the severe floods of 1948 that gave British Railways the opportunity to withdraw services between St Boswells and Duns as well as the service from Berwick to Duns. The final years of the 1960s saw the remaining routes, such as the Eyemouth branch and the Galashiels – Peebles – Edinburgh service, disappear from the railway map.

The final route to go was the Waverley line in January 1969 and, as many people no doubt remember, it did not go without a fight. Today, the only rail route in the Borders is just a short section of the east coast main line between Cockburnspath and the border crossing at Lamberton in the county of Berwick.

The yard at St Boswells.

3

Duns – Reston (Reston Junction)

Passenger service withdrawn	10 September 1951	*Stations closed*	*Date*
Distance	8¾ miles	Duns	10 September 1951
Company	North British	Edrom	10 September 1951
		Chirnside	10 September 1951

A visit by railway enthusiasts to the closed station at Duns, April 1963.

Opened in August 1849, the line from Duns to Reston was seen as an important cross-country route and its construction reflected this. For example, the line was double track rather than the single track which would normally have been installed. However, within ten years the optimistic view of the line had changed and it was reduced to single track. The line formed a through route to St Boswells on the Waverley route from Edinburgh to Carlisle via Hawick and was opened in full by 1865. The winter of 1948 was very bad, resulting in a large degree of flood damage to many rail lines in the Borders. Severe flooding between St Boswells and Duns resulted in the passenger services being suspended and they were never reinstated, although freight services continued to use the line. This meant that Duns was only served by trains from Reston on the east coast main line between Edinburgh and Berwick-upon-Tweed. Freight services lasted until 1964 and a railway special used the line in April 1963.

Eyemouth – Burnmouth (Burnmouth Junction)

Passenger service withdrawn — 5 February 1962 — *Station closed* — *Date*
Distance — 3 miles — Eyemouth — 5 February 1962
Company — North British

The station and Victoria Road, Eyemouth.

The railway came to Eyemouth in 1891 with the construction of a branch line from the east coast main line at Burnmouth. It was a great boon to the town for it brought a large number of holidaymakers, mainly from Edinburgh. Originally the line was owned by the Eyemouth Railway Company but it was acquired by the North British in 1900. Being so close to the North Sea meant that at most times of the year the line was covered in what is known as an east coast 'haar', a heavy sea fog. The terminus at Eyemouth was that of a typical branch line station and most of the journeys from here were to the nearest large town of Berwick-upon-Tweed. The severe flooding of 1948 resulted in the line being closed for nine months. Steam traction lasted to the end. Today there is no trace of the railway left.

Galashiels (Kilknowe Junction) – Rosewell and Hawthornden *

Passenger service withdrawn	5 February 1962	*Stations closed*	*Date*
Distance	37 miles	Innerleithen	5 February 1962
Company	North British	Cardrona	5 February 1962
		Peebles (first)	1 October 1864
Stations closed	*Date*	Peebles	5 February 1962
Clovenfords	5 February 1962	Earlyvale Gate	28 February 1857
Thornielee	6 November 1950	Eddleston	5 February 1962
Walkerburn	5 February 1962		

Walkerburn Station.

The railway came to Galashiels in 1849 with the construction of the line from Edinburgh to Hawick on the Waverley route. The line from Galashiels to Rosewell and Hawthornden was similar to a wide loop as it left the Waverley route at Galashiels, opening in 1866. Being quite a distance in length, the loop had a few lines radiating from it. At Peebles there was the Caledonian to Symington; at Leadburn there was the North British line to Dolphinton and from there the Caledonian line to Carstairs. The service along the route was very sparse and freight services were withdrawn at the same time as the passenger services.

* Further closed stations on the line which were in Midlothian were Leadburn, Pomathorn Halt, Rosslynlee Hospital Halt, Rosslynlee.

RAILWAY STATION,
INNERLEITHEN.

R.R.R.
E.

The 2.06 p.m. service from Galashiels to Edinburgh (via Peebles) at Cardrona, January 1962.

Eddleston Station, *c.* **1910.**

Jedburgh – Roxburgh (Roxburgh Junction)

Passenger service withdrawn	13 August 1948	*Stations closed*	*Date*
Distance	7 miles	Jedburgh	13 August 1948
Company	North British	Jedfoot	13 August 1948
		Nisbet	13 August 1948
		Kirkbank	13 August 1948

Jedburgh Station.

The Jedburgh Railway Company was responsible for the creation of this branch line which joined the line from St Boswells to Kelso and Tweedmouth at Roxburgh. Opened in July 1856, the line was worked by the North British who took full ownership four years later. The station was not very convenient for the town so in later years the company provided a connecting bus service for the hilly three quarters of a mile journey from the town centre. On 12 August 1948 torrential rain caused severe flooding which damaged the line so much that passenger services had to be withdrawn the following day. They were never reinstated. However, freight traffic continued to use the line until August 1964 and the service from St Boswells to Kelso and Coldstream continued to carry passenger traffic until June 1964.

A class D34 4-4-0, no. 62471, "Glen Falloch" with a
'Scott Country' railtour at Jedfoot, April 1959.

A class B1 4-6-0, no. 61324, passing the closed station of Nisbet with a 'Scottish Rambler' railtour, April 1963.

"Glen Falloch" with its 'Scott Country' railtour, this time at Kirkbank, April 1959.

Kershope Foot – Edinburgh (Portobello East Junction) *

Passenger service withdrawn	6 January 1969
Distance	74 miles
Company	North British

Stations closed	Date
Kershope Foot (Cumberland)	6 January 1969
Newcastleton	6 January 1969
Steele Road	6 January 1969
Riccarton Junction	6 January 1969
Shankend	6 January 1969
Stobs	6 January 1969
Hawick (first)	1 July 1862
Hawick	6 January 1969
Hassendean	6 January 1969
Belses	6 January 1969
St Boswells	6 January 1969
Newstead	October 1852
Melrose	6 January 1969
Galashiels	6 January 1969

Newcastleton Station, *c.* 1914.

This line formed the northerly section of the Waverley route from Edinburgh to Carlisle via Hawick. The Waverley was a difficult route to operate as it had severe gradients and numerous twists and curves, and consequently it became one of the first main lines in Britain to be closed. One of the remotest stations on this stretch of the route was at Riccarton Junction where the North British created a community of workers to service the line. There were about thirty cottages but no road access. The closed nature of the settlement caused friction amongst the people there and on several occasions the police had to be called to maintain law and order. The last passenger train which ran on the Waverley route was an overnight sleeper from Edinburgh Waverley to London St Pancras. At Newcastleton protesters to the closure blocked the line for more than an hour before the train could continue on its journey.

* Further closed stations on the line which were in the Lothians were Bowland, Stow, Fountainhall, Heriot, Tynehead, Fushiebridge, Gorebridge, Newtongrange, Dalhousie, Easkbank and Dalkeith, Glenesk, Millerhill, Niddrie, Niddrie Junction.

A class A3, no. 60094, leaving Steele Road Station, June 1960.

A class K1, no. 62022, departs from Riccarton Junction.

Hawick Station.

A departure from Hawick.

A class V2, no. 60808, at Hassendean Station.

Melrose Station.

A class V2, no. 60936, at Galashiels Station.

The sheds at Galashiels.

Lauder – Fountainhall Junction

Passenger service withdrawn	12 September 1932	*Stations closed*	*Date*
Distance	10¼ miles	Lauder	12 September 1932
Company	North British	Oxton	12 September 1932

Opened in 1901, this was one of several light railways in Scotland around the turn of the century. It provided a proper transport system into this part of the country and opened up the area to new trade such as anglers who were now able to get access to the large trout streams for which the region is famous. Like most light railways, passenger services did not last long, although freight services continued until 1958 and a steam passenger special travelled over the line in November that year just before it was lifted.

Leadburn (Leadburn Junction) – Dolphinton

		Stations closed	Date
Passenger service withdrawn	1 April 1933	Lamancha	1 April 1933
Distance	10 miles	Macbie Hill	1 April 1933
Company	North British	Broomlee	1 April 1933
		Dolphinton	1 April 1933

The station at Broomlee, *c.* 1912. According to the message on the postcard 'it is a nice place, well filled with visitors'.

This line was built under the ownership of the Leadburn, Linton and Dolphinton Railway Company and opened in 1864. Initially, it was purely a local affair but later it was connected to the main lines to Carlisle from Edinburgh and Glasgow. The small village of Dolphinton had two stations – one belonging to the Caledonian Railway Company and the other to the North British. Standing on the border of Peeblesshire and Lanarkshire, the village was where the Caledonian line, which ran through Lanarkshire to meet the main west coast line between Glasgow and Carlisle, met the North British line, which continued on through Peeblesshire to the Waverley route from Edinburgh to Carlisle. Attempts to have a joint station shared by both companies came to no avail and the result was two separate stations which were only a third of a mile apart. Freight services were withdrawn at the same time as passenger services and the line was lifted shortly afterwards.

The station at Dolphinton, *c.* 1913.

Riccarton Junction – Deadwater

Passenger service withdrawn   15 October 1956   *Stations closed*   *Date*
Distance   5¾ miles   Saughtree   15 October 1956
Company   North British

The closed station at Saughtree.

This section of line from Riccarton Junction on the Waverley route formed part of the line which ran into England known as the Riccarton Junction – Reedsmouth line. Opened in July 1862, the line was initially called the Border Counties Railway as it eventually reached Hexham on the Carlisle to Newcastle line. The North British obtained running powers over the North Eastern Railway route between Hexham and Carlisle and thereby allowed through trains to be operated between Edinburgh and Newcastle via the Border Counties line, but the journey time was about four and a half hours. The only station on the route which was in Scotland was Saughtree which was closed between December 1944 and August 1948. Freight services on the line lasted until September 1958.

St Boswells (Ravenswood Junction) – Duns

		Stations closed	Date
Passenger service withdrawn	13 August 1948		
Distance	22 miles	Earlston	13 August 1948
Company	North British	Gordon	13 August 1948
		Greenlaw	13 August 1948
		Marchmont	13 August 1948

Earlston Station, *c.* **1906.**

Opened in 1863, this line formed the westerly portion of the route that ran from St Boswells on the Waverley route to Reston, which stood on the east coast main line between Edinburgh and Berwick-upon-Tweed. The line had on average about four return trips between St Boswells and Berwick with the 42 mile journey taking about an hour and a half. Duns was the main town on the route and the reason for the closure of the St Boswells to Duns section in 1948 was the severe flooding which actually washed away the section from Duns to Greenlaw. The section from Duns to Reston remained open until September 1951. Freight services continued to use the line until 1965.

GORDON RAILWAY STATION
c. 1905.

"Glen Falloch" and the 'Scott Country' railtour at the closed station of Greenlaw, April 1959.

The closed station at Marchmont, 1953.

St Boswells (Kelso Junction) – Coldstream

Passenger service withdrawn	15 June 1964	*Stations closed*	*Date*
Distance	17 miles	Roxburgh	15 June 1964
Company	North British/North Eastern	Wallace Nick	27 January 1851
		Kelso	15 June 1964
Stations closed	*Date*	Sprouston	4 July 1955
Maxton	15 June 1964	Carham	4 July 1955
Rutherford	15 June 1964		

No. 67617 at Roxburgh Station.

Known as the Tweed Valley line, this route ran from St Boswells to Berwick-upon-Tweed. The border with England was at Carham and because of this the North Eastern Railway Company owned and operated the line into Scotland as far as Kelso. Only two stations were built in Scotland by this company and these were Sprouston and Carham in Roxburghshire. As the railway border was at Kelso, relations between the two companies were not very cordial as the North British felt that the North Eastern had no right to operate in Scotland. This antagonism continued right up to closure. When British Railways took over the line in 1948 the Scottish territory was stretched back to the border at Carham where appropriate border crossing signs were posted. However, timetables showed nothing east of Carham on the English side except for the arrival times at Tweedmouth just south of Berwick-upon-Tweed. During the floods of 1948 the Tweed Valley line became host to the expresses from the east coast main line which had to be diverted. This happened again in the mid-1950s but by that time local passenger levels had declined considerably. By the time of closure the annual cost of operating the line's passenger services was £60,000 while the receipts were just over £2,000. Freight services to Carham lasted until 1965 and those to Kelso from St Boswells until March 1968.

Kelso Station, September 1956.

The sheds and yard at Kelso, with the station on the extreme left, September 1956.

Selkirk – Galashiels (Galafoot Junction)

Passenger service withdrawn	10 September 1951	*Stations closed*	*Date*
Distance	6¼ miles	Selkirk	10 September 1951
Company	North British	Lindean	10 September 1951
		Abbotsford Ferry	5 January 1931

Station staff at Selkirk.

This branch line to Selkirk from Galashiels on the Waverley route opened in 1856. It was a great boost to Selkirk as it allowed easy transportation of woollen products from its mills and livestock from the many farms surrounding it. The line passed Abbotsford House, once the home of Sir Walter Scott, and a station was built at Abbotsford Ferry in the early 1900s to cater for tourists who wanted to visit the house. Although it was closed in 1931, it was reopened occasionally to transport locals back from the Braw Lads Gathering, an annual event which still takes place. In the 1920s the line had a fairly good service with around ten return trips to Galashiels per day. However, the expansion of bus services took its toll and by 1949 daily departures had decreased to just two. After closure Selkirk Station continued to sell tickets for services from Galashiels and freight services continued until November 1964.

"Glen Falloch" again, this time at the closed station of Lindean, April 1959.

Abbotsford Ferry.

Symington (Symington Junction) – Peebles *

		Stations closed	Date
Passenger service withdrawn	5 June 1950		
Distance	19 miles	Broughton	5 June 1950
Company	Caledonian	Stobo	5 June 1950
		Lyne	5 June 1950
		Peebles	5 June 1950

Broughton Station, *c.* **1908.**

This line linked Symington, on the west coast line between Carstairs and Carlisle, with Peebles on the line from Edinburgh to Galashiels. Peebles had two stations, one belonging to the Caledonian and the other to the North British. Although linked to each other by rail, a passenger service between the two over the River Tweed was never provided and passengers had to make there own way between the two stations.

* The closed stations on the line that were in Lanarkshire were Coulter and Biggar. Details of these can be found in *Lanarkshire's Lost Railways.*

The closed Caledonian station at Peebles.

Talla Reservoir (Victoria Lodge) – Rachan

Passenger service withdrawn	28 September 1905	Stations closed	Date
Distance	8 miles	Victoria Lodge	28 September 1905
Company	Edinburgh Water Board	Crook Inn	28 September 1905

This line was built to service the construction work on the reservoir which was designed to supply water to Edinburgh. The construction site in Peeblesshire was remote and the only way to gain access to it was to construct a railway from the Caledonian line between Symington and Peebles. In order to accommodate the requirements of the construction traffic, the Caledonian doubled a mile of its single track between Broughton and Rachan stations and the work began in 1895. The route taken by the line followed Talla Glen and the River Tweed to Victoria Lodge which was situated at the proposed edge of the reservoir and a platform for the workmen was built at Crook Inn, a local hostelry. Local residents were also able to use the line and, as it had been built with standard gauge, approaches were made after the reservoir was completed to keep it open. However, these came to nothing and the track was lifted by 1912.

No. 61968 at Cockburnspath Station on the line between Edinburgh and Berwick-upon-Tweed.

Closed passenger stations on lines still open to passenger services

Line/Service	**Edinburgh – Berwick-upon-Tweed ***

Station	*Date of closure*
Cockburnspath	18 June 1951
Grantshouse	4 May 1964

Station	*Date of closure*
Reston	4 May 1964
Ayton	5 February 1962
Burnmouth	5 February 1962

Grantshouse Station, *c.* 1910.

* The closed stations on this line which were in the Lothians were Jocks Lodge, Portobello, Joppa (first), Joppa, Newhailes, Inveresk, Wallyford, Seton Mains Halt, Ballencrieff, East Fortune, East Linton, Innerwick.

Station staff and taxis at Reston.

Ayton Station.

A class V2, no. 60944, southbound express livestock train at Burnmouth, July 1959.